GOLF INSTRUCTOR'S LIBRARY

TROUBLE
SHOOTING

GOLF INSTRUCTOR'S LIBRARY

TROUBLE SHOOTING

MICHAEL HOBBS

THE
APPLE
PRESS

A QUINTET BOOK

Published by The Apple Press
6 Blundell Street
London N7 9BH

ISBN 1-85076-282-1

This book was designed and produced by
Quintet Publishing Limited
6 Blundell Street
London N7 9BH

Creative Director: Terry Jeavons
Designer: Stuart Walden
Project Editor: David Barraclough
Illustrator: Rob Schone
Photographer: Michael Hobbs

Typeset in Great Britain by
Central Southern Typesetters, Eastbourne
Manufactured in Hong Kong by
Regent Publishing Services Limited
Printed in Hong Kong by
Leefung-Asco Printers Limited

Although the PGA now officially uses the term 'the
hold', this book throughout refers to 'the grip', which is
still commonly used among golfers.

CONTENTS

PREFACE

I am a left-handed golfer. However, over the years I haven't found it difficult to follow golf instruction writing, which is traditionally directed at right-handers.

As a golf writer, I know that always mentioning each form of the golfing species is easily possible, but leads to many repetitive phrases that impair the readability of the book. As a left-hander I know we have learned to cope in a 90 per cent right-handed world. A right-hander, on the other hand, is far less able. I don't think he could follow a text written for left-handers – imagine him trying to use left-handed scissors or knock in a tack, grasping the hammer left-handed. What injuries and incompetence would result for this less adaptable and accomplished sector of the human species!

ACKNOWLEDGEMENTS

Above all, I should like to thank Grenville Warne for being a splendid model for my instructional photography. He gave up many hours throughout a whole season when he would surely far rather have been playing than demonstrating. His help has been invaluable.

I should like to thank my main golf club, Tracy Park near Bristol, England, for allowing me to carry out most of the instruction photography on its splendid 27 holes. I also thank other clubs for more limited photographic facilities.

The club's professional, Grant Aitken, and his son and assistant professional Kelvin, have also been invariably helpful with advice, information and allowing me to use equipment for illustrations.

At Quintet Publishing, I should particularly like to thank David Barraclough for his continuous work throughout the project and also Peter Arnold who was responsible for the detailed copy editing. My thanks are also due to Rob Shone for his production of drawings and diagrams and the design team at Bridgewater Design.

Michael Hobbs   Worcester, England

INTRODUCTION

Golf is a cross-country game. Intended playing areas may be superbly maintained, but most of the course consists of relatively natural terrain when compared with the surfaces on which – say – tennis or bowls are played.

This means that even a perfect shot can result in difficulties (the lie of the ball, for example), and if a shot is less than perfect, we can expect to be, and very often are, in real trouble.

Some of those difficulties, such as bunkers and artificial water, are placed for precisely that purpose by the course architect – to punish a golfer for his mistakes. Others are simply the result of playing over natural ground. The situations one can find there are often, perhaps even usually, more difficult to play from than any bunker.

This book aims to cover all the trouble shots a golfer may expect to play, not just in one round, but throughout the golfing year. You can't expect to play brilliant recoveries from every predicament, but I hope you'll find at least partial solutions in these pages. That's about all we can expect in trouble shooting country.

ABOVE: Natural linksland.

CHAPTER ONE

IN SAND

Most club golfers choose clubs by the set of a dozen or so. Some, perhaps a little more thoughtful, may go so far as separating the woods from the irons and choose each category separately.

Professionals have a very different approach. The next time you are at a tournament, see if you can get a look in the pros' bags, especially those of the less-famous players. If you manage it, you are likely to see a tremendous variety of makes and models, with the only approach to uniformity appearing in the range of irons, from about 7 to 3. Every other one is likely to be regarded as a specialist club.

Every golfer selects a putter as an individual item, even if there are dozens in the collection, but the pro is out to find just that driver, 1-iron, fairway wood, couple of wedges and especially the sand iron which he eventually decides best suits his swing and his methods.

While the driver probably heads the priority list, the sand iron gets as much attention as any other.

Why is this?

BUNKERS – CHOOSING A SAND IRON

Top professionals miss a lot of greens, as a glance at the statistics published by both the US and European Tours will reveal. They show that even the best player in the 'greens in regulation' category – which means a par 3 in one, a par 4 in two and a par 5 in three – fails about 25 per cent of the time. But he doesn't miss any of them by much. So where does he finish? In the greenside bunkers, of course.

He then becomes a far more impressive golfer. One who gets down in two more than 60 per cent of the time.

No wonder the pros consider the sand iron so important and why they spend so much time selecting just the right club. You don't need to go to extremes, but it's well worth while for you to give the matter your keen consideration. You certainly shouldn't discard a good sand iron when changing a set of irons.

So just what makes a good sand iron? Let's take the main desirable characteristics first.

The most important thing to consider is the sole, and here the sand iron differs considerably from the other irons. Here, it takes the form of a heavy flange which is higher at the leading edge than the trailing edge, and it is that trailing edge which helps prevent your clubhead from digging into the sand, and encourages it to ride through instead.

This kind of club was invented by Gene Sarazen in 1931. He didn't consider himself a good sand player, and experimented with soldering lead to the sole of an iron until he had developed that higher trailing edge which enabled him to coast the clubhead through sand rather than dig down into it. The following year, Gene won both the US and British Opens and gave much of the credit to his new invention. Indeed, he had revolutionised bunker play by making the normal 'splash' shot much easier for the average player. He also enabled the very good ones to think in terms of getting much closer to the hole, or even holing out. Because of this good players no longer had to be content with simply getting out of the bunker to anywhere on the green.

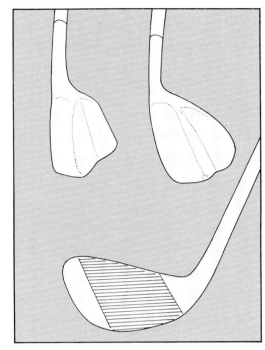

A selection of irons, with a 9-iron top left and a sand iron top right

ABOVE: Two sand irons, with the necessary higher trailing edge.

The club you choose should also be heavy. This means you really feel the clubhead throughout your swing, and can play your sand shots with less force.

In later years, people have tried to improve the sand iron. At least one of these so-called 'improvements' should be avoided.

At first sight, it would seem an obvious advantage to have a club which will do two jobs: get you out of bunkers and also be useful for pitching, the sand iron having considerably more loft than the wedge. Hence the development of the so-called 'dual purpose' sand irons.

However, the trailing edge of the sand iron makes it much more difficult to pitch with. There is always the danger that the rear edge will come into contact with the turf first, and cause the club to bounce, resulting in a thinned shot as your leading edge catches the ball around the equator.

The obvious solution was to reduce the height of the trailing edge. Certainly, you have a far better pitching club, but it doesn't work nearly as well in the sand.

So be on the lookout for any club which claims to do both jobs, and having found it – ignore it completely. It's far better to invest in a second wedge for pitching, and you really do need that high trailing edge for sand play.

Just how high the trailing edge should be depends on where you play most of your golf. Fine, soft sand demands a high trailing edge, and the actual height needed diminishes as the sand becomes coarser. Many professionals travel with two sand irons and decide which one to use when they've had a look at the bunkers.

You can't really know how well a sand iron will suit you until you try it out. You can experiment with used clubs from your pro, or borrow a few from fellow golfers until you decide on the right one. But please don't blindly accept the sand iron which comes with a new set of clubs. At least, inspect it to see if it follows the guidelines.

RIGHT: This sequence illustrates a normal splash shot. Note the relaxed address position and the fairly full backswing.

ABOVE: How the sand explodes the ball out.

GREENSIDE BUNKERS

The first consideration here is the lie of the ball. Let's start with the most simple shot; when the ball is lying cleanly, only the very bottom of it being below the surface.

Even a journeyman pro is delighted to be confronted by this shot. True – he'd rather be putting, but he will probably be much more confident of getting close to the flag from sand than from a grass lie. This contrasts sharply with the attitude of a club golfer who lacks confidence in his sand play: he will be preoccupied with how to get out, and doubtful if he can manage it at all, never mind getting close to the hole.

'Just getting out' is, in fact, the simplest part of bunker play. If you strike the sand a couple of inches or so behind the ball with your sand iron (any other lofted club will work nearly as well), and carry forcefully through with your swing, your ball will be propelled out by the displaced sand. It really is as simple as that.

TOP TO BOTTOM; LEFT TO RIGHT: A normal greenside bunker shot.

ABOVE: Never lash at a bunker shot, as here.

ABOVE: The clubhead has already overtaken the ball because the shot was topped.

Golfers fail to escape from sand for these main reasons:

A *wild 'hit and hope' swing.* Anything can happen, and probably will.

An indecisive swing. The player is simply not forceful enough to provide that explosion which blasts that ball up and out.

Swing to *the ball, not* through *it.* Perhaps the shot is forceful enough, but the clubhead is merely forced into the sand, rather than through it.

'Head up'. The fearful player doesn't really expect to get out. He looks up, at or before the strike, to see the dreaded result. Very likely, that will be a thinned shot which either catches the bunker face, or careers across the green – into more sand, probably.

Lack of precision. The basic 'splash' or 'explosion' shot is very simple, but you still have to know where to hit it, and be able to hit where you are aiming. Shots will fail if the clubhead strikes the sand too far away from the ball, or too close to it.

Playing the shot like a chip. The player is fearful of taking a full swing and being sufficiently forceful. The fear is that the ball might fly through the green. The tendency is to try to chip the ball out, a rather exact shot at the best of times. This kind of shot could well succeed from firm or wet sand, but failure is likely from a fine, soft surface.

ABOVE: The player's body has straightened up before impact. The result, here, is an air shot.

It's a useful shot to have in your armoury when playing an inland course, where, often, there is a clay underlay just beneath the sand. Here, a correctly played sand iron may bounce, and the ball is in danger of flying far beyond the green from a full shot. That kind of disaster can be avoided by playing a chip.

ABOVE: The basic 'splash' shot. Precision is the key.

ABOVE: Clubhead impact with the sand was too far behind the ball. The sand explosion has moved the ball but it has travelled only a small distance and more sideways than forwards.

15

GOLF INSTRUCTOR'S LIBRARY: TROUBLE SHOOTING

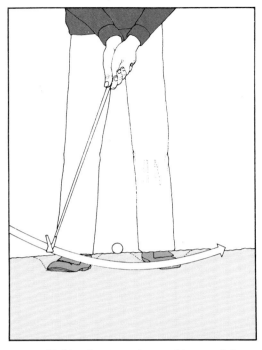

ABOVE: Sinking feet into the sand brings club arc below ball.

GETTING OUT

The first thing to do is to settle your feet firmly down into the sand. This gives you two useful advantages: your feet are firmly anchored, and your club arc is brought lower, roughly where you want it, which is beneath the ball, instead of level with it.

Although the recommendation is to hit the sand about two inches behind the ball, moderate players can minimise the chance of topping the ball by aiming to enter the sand a little further back, say, four to six inches.

The only answer is to practise until you have established a distance that suits you. Let's assume it turns out to be about four inches behind the ball, which will always allow you to take a full backswing and swing freely through the ball. You can then vary that distance by swinging more and less forcefully, and as you gain confidence, you can begin to make your strike closer to the ball.

ABOVE AND RIGHT: There was good height on this shot, which reduces run.

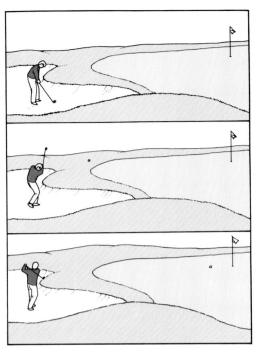

ABOVE: Note the full follow through.

SHORT SHOTS

Short shots are obviously needed when the flag is close to the greenside bunker – or anyway, quite close. You will inevitably get little backspin, so you can only hope to get your ball close to the hole by correct strength. Height on the ball will create a soft landing, and minimise run.

Stand open, so that you are aiming well to the left of your target. Also, keep the blade of your sand iron well open, but square with a line from ball to hole. The ball should be further forward in your stance than usual, about opposite the left instep.

Try to swing up and down on a fairly steep plane, which will help you gain height. If you take a shallow cut of sand under the ball, both backspin and height will increase, but you'll find that much more precision is needed than when your club enters the sand well behind the ball.

LONGER SHOTS

Longer shots are necessary when the flag is at the far side of the green, or when the bunker is, say, twenty or thirty yards short of the putting surface.

This time, take a more shallow swing, so that clubhead momentum is less killed because the clubhead is travelling forwards, rather than downwards, and propels sand at the ball more strongly.

This time you'll find that the ball will travel further if you set up square to your target, and keep the clubface square through the ball. Once again, the nearer your strike is to the ball, the more distance you will get.

A long shot from the rear of a bunker.

TOP, MIDDLE AND ABOVE: For this longer shot, the blade is squared and the stance less open.

BACKSPIN

When watching a tournament on TV, you will sometimes be amazed by the amount of backspin a professional gets on a bunker shot. This happens when the player takes the ball directly, without sand intervening between ball and clubface.

However, the pro rarely does this when the flag is near. The shot is reserved for a bunker which is some way short, or wide of, a green. The sand iron is not necessarily the club to use; a wedge, 9-iron and so on may well be preferable.

You can also expect to achieve more backspin from wet sand. Once again, you might try to take the ball directly, avoiding the sand iron because the trailing edge of the flange on the sole of your club may well meet the sand first, and cause the club to bounce. A thinned shot is then the likely result. The relatively sharp leading edges of a wedge or 9-iron will cut into the sand, rather than bounce.

These clubs are also safer to use when your feet tell you that the ground is hard immediately before the top layer of sand, a condition found all too often in badly maintained or constructed bunkers, and usually occurring on inland courses. Once again, by using a wedge or 9-iron you avoid the danger of bounce from the harder clay soil or other material.

This action shot from the bunker clearly shows how much sand is taken.

As the ball is lying on wet sand a 9-iron or wedge are the clubs to use.

Successful bunker play depends upon a good stance and the taking of
sand before the ball. Note the divot mark runs parallel to the player's
stance because a longer shot has been played.

BURIED LIES

You will only experience a buried lie when your ball *runs* into a bunker if it does so at speed into soft, fine sand. More often, it arises when your ball has pitched directly into sand, and lies in its pitch mark. On average, about half the ball will lie below the level of the sand, but this very much depends on the firmness of the sand involved. If it's very fine and soft, your ball can disappear altogether.

When playing a bunker shot from a buried lie, you can forget all about the basic sand shot rule of playing with an open blade: impact with the greater body of sand involved is likely to open it even more, providing no real explosion of sand to move the ball on and out.

In fact, there are two quite different ways of playing this type of shot. In the first, you square your blade, play the ball further back in your stance – somewhere about the middle – and then swing far more forcefully than you would for the standard splash shot. You also need to hold your club more firmly than usual, trying to maintain the square face through the impact zone.

Many players fail with this shot simply because they don't swing forcefully enough, worrying perhaps, that they will send the ball many yards through the green. Unless you hit very close to the ball, there's very little danger of that, however.

Unfortunately, you'll get no backspin at all. Your ball will fly low, and because of that, run further than usual. So what's your answer if the flag is quite near the bunker? There isn't

ABOVE: The balls lie in their own pitch marks.

one. This is one trouble shot which has no complete answer. Remember – your main aim is to get out of the sand, not get down in two.

Of course, if the hole is at the far side of the green, your troubles decrease. A mixture of good judgement and a little luck may well get you close to your target.

The second method requires you to keep the clubhead square through the stroke by holding the club with the toe turned in, and then swinging as before. The idea is that the turned-in toe makes it much less likely for the clubhead to be forced open through the ball.

Some players use neither of these methods. They use an open face as usual, being confident that they can maintain this position through impact. This is much more dangerous, and may result in your ball travelling a few yards and remaining in the sand. However, there is a better chance of more height on the shot, and therefore less run.

Low flight is, of course, a major problem. Excessive run is one thing, but you have to get out of the bunker first, and how do you do that if your flight isn't high enough?

The answer is quite simple. You don't. You may have to be content to try and escape, and if necessary, accept the penalty of having to play from the sand again if you fail. This time, however, you'll probably have a better lie.

If your bunker isn't particularly deep, but you are confronted by a steep face, take a look around. You may have to abandon all thoughts of playing for the flag and content yourself with escape from the sand, playing out sideways – or even backwards. This will probably mean the loss of a stroke, but that's one hundred per cent better than losing two.

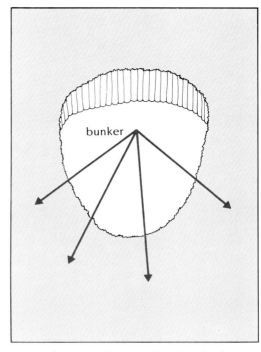

ABOVE: Play out sideways or backwards when the face of the bunker is very steep.

ABOVE: Squared blade, ball back in stance.

ABOVE: Using plenty of clubhead speed.

ABOVE: When playing out of a bunker keep your head down.

ABOVE: Bunker situations where quick height is needed.

THE DOWNHILL LIE

This situation arises when your ball has run into sand with very little pace on it, stopping quickly on the slope down to the middle found in most bunkers.

The danger is that your clubhead will skate over the sand and strike the ball directly, or even thin it. You can reduce this peril by squaring up the blade and playing the ball further back in your stance. From the back of a bunker, you won't often need much height, so you can afford to play with a square club face.

ABOVE: Playing from a downhill lie.

THE UPHILL LIE

Here, your ball will probably have been travelling at speed when it ran into the sand, running on up the face. When playing this shot, you must be wary of striking too far behind the ball, which would entail trying to explode a substantial body of sand at it. This would probably result in a loss of sufficient impetus to move the ball very far.

Obviously enough, the answer is to make your club enter the sand a little closer to the ball, and, as usual, swing firmly through the sand.

ABOVE: Playing from an uphill lie.

DIFFICULT BUNKER STANCES

When your ball is only a short distance into the sand, you may be unable to stand to the ball with both feet in the bunker. This means that your two feet are going to be at significantly different levels.

You probably won't have much difficulty keeping your balance when standing still, but just wait until you try swinging at the ball!

There's no clear solution, and a high-precision shot will probably be impossible, for you or anyone else. However, there's nothing to stop you rehearsing the shot a few times, practising the swing until you have an indication how forcefully you can swing without losing balance before or at impact. Please feel free to fall over afterwards!

Weigh up the shot and assess your chances of success. If the shot then seems impossible, settle for escape and play out away from the flag.

ABOVE AND RIGHT: Playing from an awkward stance.

UNDER THE FRONT LIP

Quite often, a bunker has an overhanging lip of turf. It's vital to prevent your ball fizzing into this, because it could well plug into the soil, rendering your next shot impossible. It would mean shifting your ball, and a sizeable chunk of turf, onto the green.

Open the club face more than usual, trying for maximum height to get the ball soaring quickly. Swing steeply, both back and down, again hoping to gain maximum height.

ABOVE: Plugged in the face. You will have to blast out ball and soil.

A BARE LIE

Most golfers rake the sand towards them as they retreat after playing their shot. The end result is that, over a period of time, sand becomes more shallow at the centre of the bunker than it is at the edges. Eventually, you get fairly bare lies in the middle, and that condition persists until the bunker is dug out and new sand laid.

Give up any idea of using a sand iron with a high trailing edge, because bounce is likely. Regard the shot as a short pitch, and take the ball clean, using a wedge or 9-iron. If you aren't comfortable with this sort of shot, don't swing too gently.

Any lack of precision in the strike will mean that you won't get the ball out. Play the shot reasonably firmly, accepting that your ball may travel further beyond the hole than you would like.

ABOVE: Rake towards the middle of the bunker.

ABOVE: This bare lie is the result of the wind.

ABOVE: Fairway bunkers are so placed to 'catch' anything but the best of shots. Fortunately, with the lie of the ball in this bunker there would not be too much difficulty in playing the next shot.

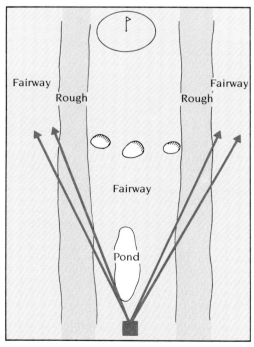

ABOVE: It is not against the rules to play to another fairway to avoid hazards. However, before taking this option make sure the adjacent fairway is clear of players.

FAIRWAY BUNKERS

When Severiano Ballesteros won his first major Championship, the British Open at Royal Lytham and St Anne's, the number of times he found bunkers caused comment. Royally, Seve declared that it hadn't mattered because "I am the best bunker player".

A few years later, on the Old Course at St Andrews, he became Champion again. It was probably the most consistent performance of his illustrious career, and was, to some extent, based on a strategy of keeping out of bunkers. Indeed, the Spaniard was quite prepared to drive to the fairway of adjacent holes, giving him difficult lines into the greens, just to make sure he did so.

So why such opposing strategies for tackling two different courses?

At Royal Lytham, Seve was mainly catching greenside bunkers and, as we have seen, today's professionals expect to get close to the hole if the ball is lying well in sand. He was confident in getting down in two more. In contrast, at St Andrews he was worried about fairway bunkers, and these can vary dramatically from course to course.

The Old Course has quite deep pot bunkers, from which a player, no matter how skilful, simply can't recover. He is content simply to escape, never mind fly his ball to a green 200 yards away.

There was a contrasting situation in the 1988 US Masters at Augusta National. Sandy Lyle needed to par the final hole to get himself into a sudden-death play-off with Mark Calcavecchia, and took an iron from the tee, aiming to drop short of a fairway bunker on the left.

He struck the ball with just a little draw, went further than he expected, and found the bunker anyway. Was Lyle downcast? Not a bit of it. He saw that his ball was lying cleanly, and not too close to the face, so he could go for the green with a 7-iron. Recovery was entirely possible, even though great precision of strike was needed if he were to whisk the ball off the surface without taking sand.

As all the world knows, Lyle did better than par. That 7-iron was truly struck, soared over the flag, and the backspin took it back towards the hole. The putt went down, and he was Masters Champion.

Bunkers don't come much tougher than the 'Hell bunker' on the 14th
Fairway at St Andrews which catches the second shot to the green.
This bunker probably cost Gene Sarazen the chance of winning the 1933
British Open.

Another of the many bunkers at St Andrews. This one is a fairway 'pot
bunker' and is difficult to see until close up to. Many unsuspecting
golfers fall foul of such bunkers.

ABOVE: No chance of making great distance from a deep fairway bunker.

DEEP FAIRWAY BUNKERS

These reduce all good golfers to around the same level. No one can recover from them and hit a distant green.

All you can do is concentrate on getting out, and being sure of landing in a good position for your next shot. There's no point at all in knocking your ball into another trap. It also makes sense to aim for a target of some sort, just as you would from a greenside bunker. This could be a flat area of fairway, or a position which gives you a good approach to the flag. You could also consider a spot which will enable you to hit a favourite club with plenty of backspin.

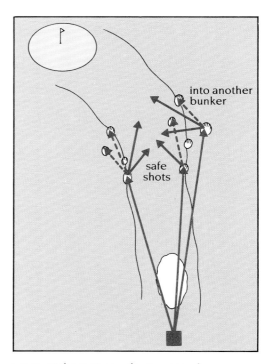

ABOVE: Make sure you don't escape from one bunker into another.

RECOVERY SHOTS

You've made a mistake and hit sand. To 'recover', in this context, means to play a sand shot which leaves you in a position as good as you would have been in if you hadn't found the bunker in the first place. This is usually possible only if your ball is lying clean, and not too close to the front face or any of the lips.

If there's no face at all, but just the front lip of a very shallow bunker, then your problems are less severe: you don't have to calculate how much loft your club should have to make sure of getting out. If there is a face, you need to visualise the trajectories you will get from various clubs. Having done that – take one more for safety, because if you fail to escape you'll be in a worse position than ever, close up to the face, or even plugged into it.

Settle your feet firmly into the sand, and shorten your grip on the club. This helps compensate for the fact that your feet are below the level of the ball, and the shortened shaft gives you a more precise strike. Don't overswing going back, because your stance is less secure on sand than it would be on turf. Swing normally, concentrating, even more than usual, on finding the back of the ball with the middle of the clubhead.

This avoids two potential disasters when playing sand shots: catching the sand just behind the ball, and thinning the shot. The first produces a very weak result, losing a great deal of distance, and perhaps even keeping you in the bunker. The second is usually caused by sheer anxiety, making you look up before you hit.

Your choice of club is wide open. Given a good strike, a 3-wood can be played successfully, and so can a long iron, but don't forget that longer shafts are more demanding on your precision.

The answer lies in experiment and practice. You may learn that you can't really trust yourself with anything more demanding than a 5-iron, let's say. So you accept the limitation, and you'll find you can still go for the green quite often, and if you're bunkered on the tee from a par 5, you'll still gain useful distance.

There is a tendency to get one club less distance from sand, and also to fade the ball. Just make allowances.

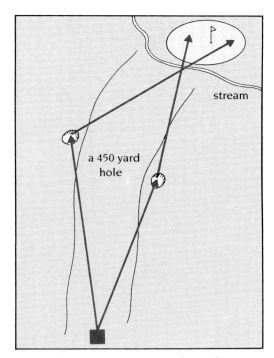

ABOVE: These are true recovery shots. The player is on the green in two.

ABOVE: The ball is sitting up on the sand, well away from the front lip. A long recovery shot should be possible.

ABOVE: From this good lie, a 3-wood could be played but this front lip might catch the ball.

35

RULES AND BEHAVIOUR IN SAND

I happen to believe that bunkers should punish a poor shot. That's what they're there for. Pine Valley, is an example of an attitude which I admire – that a bunker should sometimes be an unraked wilderness, and expanse designed to fill a golfer with apprehension.

Oakmont also used to be an example of terror bunkers – but they don't do it right any more. Until recent years they had a device which raked bunkers into a series of furrows, rather than into a level surface. There was hardly a ball which didn't nestle down into a trough. All you could expect of an Oakmont bunker was what today's golfers would call a 'bad lie'. You could get your ball out, but full recovery shots were seldom possible.

"Fine," say I. Every golfer expects to lose a shot when in the water, so why should sand be any different?

I accept that I'm in a minority, and I don't carry on a one-man protest movement by refusing to rake the sand over when I've played my shot – but many golfers do, especially if they haven't recovered well. Why should the next fellow not suffer too?

ABOVE: A grass island in a bunker isn't part of the hazard.

ABOVE: The club has been grounded.

ABOVE: As this is a practice bunker it is less frequently raked, so you have more chance to practise your recovery shots.

ABOVE: According to the rules of golf, man-made objects may be moved, if they impede your shot.

ABOVE: Look at the local rules before removing stones.

After you've played your shot, do use the rake usually provided to efface your sand divot and your footmarks. If you are really concerned about maintaining, and even improving, course conditions, don't be content with raking the sand out from the middle out to the edges as you retreat. That's what the rest of the world does, and it leads to the condition discussed under 'Bare Lies', where the sand becomes more shallow towards the centre than at the edges. Push sand towards the middle, rather than dragging it to the edge.

Sometimes, you won't be able to find a rake, but don't just shrug your shoulders and walk on. Smooth the surface with your feet as you retreat – much more effective than using your sand iron.

If there is a rake, you must remember to replace it. Sometimes there's no problem because a rake holder is provided. If not, note the custom at the course you're playing. Some seem to prefer rakes to be parked close by the bunker, others in the sand itself.

The second alternative would seem more logical: a rake left in the sand can neither divert a ball into the bunker, or prevent it from going in.

Remember the rules about grounding your club. You aren't allowed to ground your club in any hazard, and a bunker is certainly one of these. However, the grassy banks surrounding most bunkers aren't part of the hazard, and neither is any timber shoring, so you don't incur a penalty if you touch them, something all too easy to do during your backswing. A grass island in the bunker itself doesn't count as a hazard, either.

You are always allowed to move any loose impediments interfering with your shot, anywhere on a golf course – except in a hazard. So don't bend down and pick up any leaf, twig or stone which you'd like out of the way. There can be exceptions, however. Tournament professionals, for example, are allowed to pamper themselves more than we ordinary mortals, and may usually pick up stones. Even they can sometimes find themselves penalised for doing so when playing in an event such as an Open Championship not covered by the slightly modified rules used on the US and European Tours.

Your scorecard can sometimes give you a pleasant surprise. If a stone is interfering with your shot, you will sometimes find a local rule allowing you to lift it.

There is also relief without penalty from scrapes and holes in sand made by burrowing animals. You are allowed a free drop, just so long as you stay in the bunker. The same is true of casual water.

Again, sometimes a bunker may be undergoing repair, and is marked as 'GUR'. In this case you are allowed to drop without penalty. In all these cases of relief, you are not allowed, of course, to drop nearer the hole.

You are not allowed to clear sand away from your ball in order to identify it, even if you find it half buried. This isn't quite so severe as it sounds, because there is no penalty for playing the wrong ball, in this case. Have a look at it once you are out of the sand, and if it turns out to be the wrong one, retrace your steps and play again.

But what if you can't even find the ball, yet you are absolutely certain you saw it plummet down into the sand? Here you have two alternatives. You can institute a search with no penalty for touching the sand, but once a ball has been detected, it must be played without removing all the sand you might like in order to make sure it's yours. If, in spite of all the searching, the ball cannot be found, even though you 'know' the ball is in the bunker, you just have to declare it lost and retrace your steps to play your shot again under stroke and distance penalty.

It's a hard world, but at least this is only likely to occur in the finest of coastal sand.

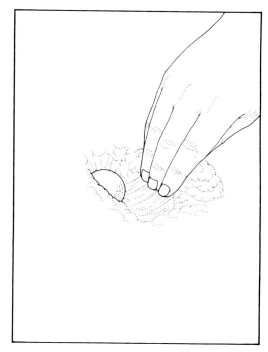

ABOVE: Once you see the ball, you aren't allowed to remove sand to identify it.

IN THE ROUGH

There are two distinct types of rough. The grass can be *long*, or it can be *dense*.
Grass which is long need not be a problem if it's thin and wispy. It may tend to wrap around your blade, but this won't usually prevent you playing an effective shot. Contrast that with the experiences at the 1990 US PGA Championship, where the rough was deep in a different sense, and balls became buried in it when only just off the greens and fairways. If it hadn't been for the presence of marshals and spectators, many more balls would have been lost, even though they resulted from shots which were by no means poor ones.

TOP: Long grass wraps around the club.

ABOVE: The ball is buried although the grass is only about 2 inches long.

ABOVE: Spectators and marshals find many errant balls.

IN DEEP ROUGH

It is reported that the editor of a well-known magazine dropped his watch while adjusting it, and took a long time to find it – just off the green.

From this kind of rough it's often impossible to play a recovery shot. Even steely-wristed professionals find they need too much strength to cut through the grass, and then *force* the ball through for any substantial distance. The only remedy is to accept the loss of a shot, select a highly lofted club in order to gain height quickly and move the ball back into play – perhaps only 50 or 100 yards onwards.

When your ball is a long way off line, and therefore far from the fairway, you may have to accept no gain in distance at all, and play out sideways.

Club choice has to vary, according to the severity of the lie. In the worst situations, the sand iron, with its extra weight and maximum loft, is the club to use. In fact, you need loft

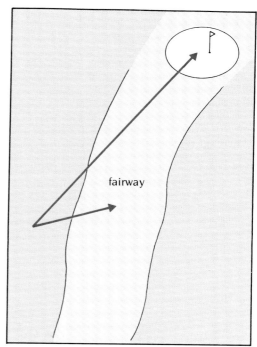

ABOVE: When the ball is in very dense or long grass, play back to the fairway instead of to the green.

ABOVE: You can get out of this but not make a full recovery.

ABOVE AND RIGHT: Getting out with a sand iron.

ABOVE AND RIGHT: Sometimes you have to play back to the fairway (the green is extreme right).

more than anything else in order to get the ball out of the clinging grass quickly, so you should never use a straight-faced club once your ball is in an unfavourable lie.

You will also tend to close the face of the club as you force through to the ball, and longer irons then become totally ineffective. Arnold Palmer found this out when playing in the 1966 US Open at Olympic.

In the final round, he was heading for a new Championship scoring record. Only Billy Casper was in any sort of contact, and he was several shots behind.

Then Palmer tried a long iron from dense rough, and his ball died in as bad a position, not many yards further on. In the end, Caspar overhauled him, and Palmer never won another major Championship. He probably still thinks how different things might have been if he'd used a wedge, rather than an iron, that day.

The tendency for the face to close in the impact zone can be counteracted if you set up the clubface more open than usual before gripping. You will also need to grip more firmly than usual, and maintain that firmness through the ball. Strength isn't usually as important as clubhead speed in the game of golf, but this is one occasion when sheer brawn is useful.

BURIED LIES IN ROUGH

You also need strength to maintain the grip and fast hands to get you out of buried lies in the grass. Many players, in this situation, are far too optimistic. They visualise the perfect result, and forget that they can't always achieve this, even from good lies, so do be realistic in assessing your chances. It pays to make sure of moving your ball out to a position where you can resume playing the hole.

Sometimes, even this isn't possible, as Ben Hogan found when playing the 1955 US Open, again at Olympic.

He was playing off with the unknown, Jack Fleck, over 18 holes, and was trying for a record fifth Open Championship as well. At the last, he played a quick hook from the tee, and landed in very dense rough. Using a lofted club, and aiming only to get back to the fairway, he needed three attempts, being able to move his ball only for short distances each time. Once there, he got down with an iron to the green and one putt – which shows how important it is to get into a position where you can continue to play the hole.

Hogan was one stroke behind Fleck playing this short par 4 hole, so couldn't afford an option he might have taken earlier in the play-off. (Fleck was well down the fairway, and there was no reason why he shouldn't make his par 4.)

He could have declared his ball unplayable, and then walked back, as far as he liked, until he found more favourable ground to drop his ball. I remember watching Tom Weiskopf doing this at the only major Championship he ever won, the 1973 British Open at Troon. He hit one drive which finished well down in the gorse, a position which gave him a fair chance of getting his ball back to the fairway – but a fair chance of failure, too. Tom decided that the risks weren't acceptable, and he picked up his ball under penalty and walked back, perhaps 100 yards, until he came upon a good lie.

Although a 6 went on his card, it could have been much worse, and a day later he was Champion. You couldn't say that that decision won him his Championship, but the wrong one could certainly have lost it for him.

OPPOSITE: These shots pose many problems. Getting the clubhead through all that grass is the biggest problem which is why it is best to select the heaviest club in your bag – a wedge or 9-iron. You won't get much distance but you should, hopefully, get out of trouble.

ABOVE AND RIGHT: When the ball is well down, use a lofted club.

SEMI-ROUGH

In US and European Tour events, as well as top amateur matches, rules are laid down concerning the length to which semi-rough should be cut. But, as I have just stressed, density of grass is far more important. Lies found in semi-rough can vary enormously.

Your ball can be sitting up as if on a tee peg, and from such a lie you can use a driver more easily than a good fairway lie. On the other hand, it may be nestling down at the roots, and a wedge back into play may well be the most sensible club selection.

You will, however, encounter conditions as extreme as this very seldom, perhaps only when grass growth is at its peak. So ignore the term 'semi-rough' and think solely about how your ball is situated. As I've said, a driver could be appropriate, if you need distance, and you can always consider taking a wood, even though you might eventually decide against it.

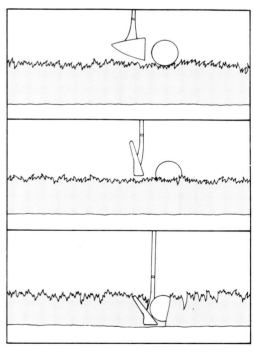

TOP: If the ball is perched on the grass, you can play another wood.

ABOVE CENTRE: The ball is only a little down in the grass so a long iron is possible.

BOTTOM: When the ball is in long grass you need a sand iron.

In the semi-rough a wood may be used if the ball is sitting up well on the grass.

A 7 being used from a reasonable lie.

When you need a long shot, there are some easy decisions to be made. A wooden clubhead pushes its way through grass, while an iron cuts through. Once you decide a wood isn't safe, you certainly shouldn't be thinking of – for example – a 3– or 4–iron. Your decision and your choice of club should be far more drastic. Think in terms of no less a degree of loft than 6.

Another useful club to have in your bag is a wood with a small head; a number 5, perhaps, or even the less-often seen number 7. These small-headed clubs are splendid for getting through grass, even moderately dense. They also make a useful substitute for players who aren't really happy with long irons at any time.

It is possible to use long irons from the semi-rough, depending on the lie. However, for most people they should be avoided at all costs, unless the lie of the ball offers no problems at all.

ABOVE: A wood pushes through the grass.

ABOVE: An iron has to cut through the grass.

ABOVE: The size of wooden clubheads can vary enormously.

ABOVE: Playing an iron from a good lie in the semi-rough.

BAD LIES IN THE ROUGH

As I've said earlier, you have to be prepared to sacrifice distance towards the green, and settle for playing out sideways. Sometimes, even this isn't an option and you take a penalty drop in kinder country. If you find you have a bad lie, but still think you can move your ball back to the fairway, how do you play the shot?

The answer is something like that for a bunker shot. Open the face before gripping, to compensate for the tendency for the face to close around impact, and play with a steeper swing arc, breaking the wrists early. Almost automatically, you will then swing back to the ball more steeply, and your ball should rise quickly, helping you to get up and clear of the grass.

An open face is essential if you want the ball to clear the grass.

THE FLYER

The normal way to play an iron shot squeezes the ball between clubhead and turf. This promotes backspin, but also reduces the speed of the ball. When your ball is resting on grass, and therefore is raised off the ground, this squeezing effect can't happen. You are whisking it off the grass, and the result is a considerably longer shot: backspin is reduced, and there is no friction between clubhead, ball and turf.

Only experience can teach you just how much further your ball will travel, and no one can ever be totally sure.

Seve Ballesteros had to use this kind of judgement and experience when playing the 17th, or Road Hole, at the Old Course at St Andrews, arguably golf's most difficult par hole.

It happened at the climax of the 1984 British Open, when Seve and Tom Watson were level. The Spaniard drove down into the left rough, when the only way to make a second shot along the line of the green possible is to drive close to out-of-bounds on the right.

But Seve had to come in from the side, and had only a few yards to play with, because a little short would have landed him in the Road bunker. Getting down in two from there is unlikely, because the flag is always set close to it in Championships. A touch too strong, and his ball would have run on into the road along the right of the green.

He examined his lie, and decided it was a flying one. Instead of selecting, say, a 4–iron, he took a 6. The shot was exact for distance, and had enough backspin to hold the green. About a quarter of a hour later he was Champion.

It had been a superb shot – but luck also smiled on him.

That's one kind of flyer. The second is quite different. When your ball is in semi-rough, or perhaps in longer grass, it can often lie with only the top half exposed. When your club meets the ball, there will be a cushion of grass in between. You can easily see just how much, when you examine the lie.

This cushion has two effects. When there are just a few blades between clubface and ball it will make little difference to the speed at which ball leaves clubhead – but backspin is considerably reduced.

Because backspin causes the ball to climb, you will have only the loft given by the angle of the clubface to rely on. Reduced backspin when the ball comes to earth will mean far less bite, and your ball will therefore run further.

Only experience of playing similar shots over months and years with the same club will tell you just how much further.

Playing from rough of any kind usually leaves grass remains compacted into the grooves on your club. Wet grass can clean them out, or in dry conditions, a little scraping with a tee peg will partly do the job.

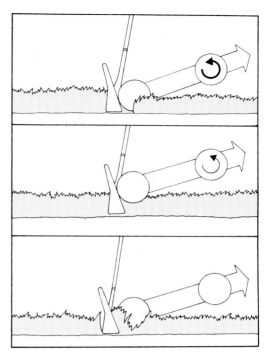

TOP: The club squeezes the ball against the turf, causing good backspin.

ABOVE CENTRE: The ball is resting on the grass, so there is little backspin.

BOTTOM: There is no backspin when grass comes between the ball and the clubface.

ABOVE: The grooves of the iron can be cleaned with a tee peg.

LEFT: The Road bunker at St Andrews. Seve had to fly it but not run across the narrow green into the road beyond. (In championship play, the flag is always set near the Road bunker. Here it is towards the front of the green.)

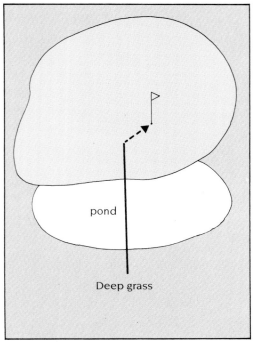

ABOVE: When lobbing from deep grass allow for side spin.

BELOW AND OPPOSITE: Playing the lob. Notice the open stance and that the clubhead is cutting across the ball parallel to the feet.

DEEP OR THICK ROUGH BY THE GREENSIDE

So far, we have been considering playing techniques and options when the aim is either to escape, or to play to a green some considerable distance away. If, however, you're in this kind of trouble just a few yards from the putting surface, you aren't usually going to be satisfied with merely hacking it out. You'll want to be on the green, preferably close to the hole and so you must consider the options available.

The main problem is that grass intervening between ball and clubhead will deprive you of backspin. So in this case it is recommended that you substitute height, with the result that your ball plummets *downwards* rather than *forwards* when it pitches.

To achieve this, you play the lob, which is rather like a bunker splash shot. Open the stance, stand with the ball opposite your left instep, and set the clubface open, aiming at the flag, or even a little to the left, to take into account the left-to-right sidespin you should get. Take a bunker-length backswing – about three-quarters – and swing freely through the hitting area.

Things become even more like a bunker shot when you don't think you can get your clubhead to the ball directly. Aim to make contact a few inches behind the ball, and add a little more swing pace, enabling your club to slide through the resistance offered by the grass.

This is not as difficult to play as the cut-up shot from a good fairway lie, because that needs great strike precision. Because you should get the ball up and out quickly, you won't be left woefully contemplating a ball which has moved just a foot or two, smothered by grass.

You don't always have to play the lob from long greenside grass. If you have a clear path into your ball, and a reasonable lie, play a normal short pitch with a lofted club.

ABOVE AND RIGHT: Playing the lob from a better lie. The open stance and follow through remain the same.

LOOSE LIES

Golf balls often come to rest on loose divots, leaves, pine needles, small twigs and other moveable objects. The operative word here is 'moveable'. Outside of bunkers, you can pick up and toss away anything which impedes your stroke or – particularly when putting or chipping – which your ball may strike later on. When this material is not too close to the ball, there's no real problem, although you do have to be careful that the material is dead and not growing material still attached to the ground. You are not allowed, under the rules of the game, to pull up wispy grass by the roots.

Because someone hasn't replaced a divot this player is now faced with an awkward shot which requires a lofted club. To make sure you are never faced with this shot, replace divots. This way eventually this sort of shot will be eliminated.

You can't avoid falling leaves and if your ball lands on one it is unfortunate. Because the removal of the leaf would cause your ball to move you have to play the shot as it lies.

This stone is a 'moveable' object under the rules but you must make sure your ball does not move in the process of removing it.

Moving the leaf would cause the ball to move which is not allowed.

Moving this twig would cause the ball to move which is not allowed.

Because the tree is marked, a drop without penalty is permitted.

Your judgement has to come into play once such objects are closer to the ball. Even if you are still some distance away and tread on one end of a twig, which then moves and in turn moves the ball – that's a penalty. So tread carefully.

Once you get to the ball, examine material which might affect your shot. Most important is anything you will strike before impact with the ball. Even a small twig, intervening between clubface and ball at impact can cause a disaster. Get rid of such things – but first make sure your ball doesn't move as a result.

The dangers of inadvertently moving your ball are still not quite over. You have yet to take your stance and address the ball. Causing the ball to move when grounding your club close to it is always a possibility. So, if there's a danger here – don't ground your club. This isn't a new situation, because you already avoid grounding when in a bunker or in water.

Some golfers never ground clubs, believing that this prevents touching the turf at the beginning of a backswing, and avoids a tendency to lift the club at the start.

Those fallen leaves (and twig) again! This time they are easily removed but take care when doing so.

When playing from this lie you have to make contact with the leaf before the ball.

Having taken all these precautions – which takes much longer to write about than actually to do when out on the course – you must then make small adjustments to the way you play the shot. Precision is the main thing: you need to whisk the ball off the loose surface, rather than hitting down on to that cushion of leaves or pine needles. This isn't a situation for a full-out shot: grip a little lower down and swing easily, concentrating on an exact strike, rather than on clubhead speed.

You can usually ignore objects which your ball will contact immediately after impact. A ball brushing a leaf aside won't be much affected. It's rather different, however, when the leaves come before the ball, because they will cushion the shot and deprive you of some backspin. Make allowances. These situations won't happen all that often in a golfing lifetime, so you won't have experience to draw upon. Rely on your imagination to tell you how the ball will behave.

If anything is still growing then you cannot remove it. The simple rule is: If it's dead then it can be removed, provided it doesn't cause your ball to move.

RULES AND BEHAVIOUR IN THE ROUGH

Rough, though it may be punishing, isn't classed as a hazard under the rules of golf, so there are no special rules to worry about.

This means that you are allowed to identify your ball positively, and are penalised if you fail to do so and play the wrong ball. You are permitted to move the grass in order to do so, but must not improve your lie.

Be careful how you address your ball. Causing it to move costs one penalty stroke, so it's wise to avoid grounding your club if there's any chance of this happening. But what does 'moving the ball' mean?

It means making the ball move from its original position, and coming to rest in another one. This may be just a fraction of an inch, but if your ball merely rocks and settles back into its original position, then that does not constitute movement in golf, and there's no penalty.

If your ball is so deeply entangled that you judge there is no chance of moving it, even with a sand iron, you can, any time, anywhere on the course, declare it unplayable. This leaves you with three options. The first is to take your penalty drop within two club lengths, and no nearer the hole.

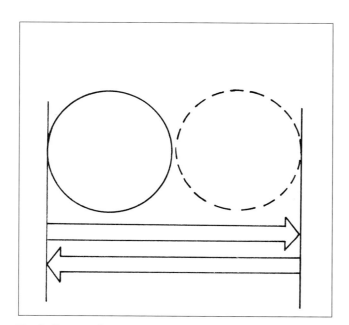

The ball moves but returns to its original position, therefore there is no penalty.

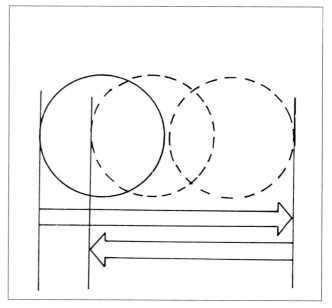

When the ball oscillates but comes to a lie a fraction of an inch away from its original position, you have to take the penalty.

ABOVE: You can choose a drop if you decide a shot is unplayable.

However, as you survey the local scene, you could well decide that such a drop would leave you in an equally unpromising situation. You might finish in just as difficult a lie – but without the option of trying again, except with the loss of another penalty shot. If so, you can walk back to the tee, or to any other place from which you struck the ball, and play your shot again, under penalty.

However, you can save distance by taking the third option. Walk back, keeping your lie between you and the hole, until you find a suitable place to drop.

IN WATER

When your ball finishes in water, you normally have no problem at all. It's a lost ball, or an irretrievable one, and you just have to accept your one stroke penalty and play on with no pause for thought.

At other times, it will be in clear sight, and decision time. Do you play a shot or retrieve your ball? There is at least one case on record where the decision to play was taken rather to extremes.

In around 1912, a player in the qualifying round of the Shawnee Invitational for Ladies at Shawnee-on-Delaware, Pennsylvania, sent her tee shot, at the short 16th, into the Binniekill River – and it floated. Her husband, rather sadistically you might say, bundled her into a boat and took the oars.

ABOVE: If it's in the middle, accept your penalty shot.

TOP AND ABOVE: Drop another and play on.

When playing a short shot over water play
it like a lob, making sure the stance is
open.

She eventually got the boat ashore after a multitude of attemps a mile-and-a-half downstream, and then had to play through a wood on her way back to the fairway. She eventually sank her putt, having taken 166 strokes. Not bad for a 130-yard hole!

I'm not suggesting you go to those extremes. Indeed, one decision you must make when your ball is in water is whether you are willing to risk injury or not. Water is hard stuff when you swing a golf club into it at speed, and hand or wrist injury is quite likely if you attempt to play a forceful shot through it.

There's probably no point in taking the risk, however. The water will slow your clubhead speed by a considerable amount, and there will also be a similar effect on the ball. Even if your clubhead does have significant momentum left when it meets the ball, escape proves impossible because of the water's resistance to the ball itself.

The rule of thumb must be – don't attempt to play out of water if the whole of the ball is below the surface. The chances of injury are substantial, and of success negligible. Take your penalty drop: it's only one stoke.

You may remember Payne Stewart playing the last hole at The Belfry, at the end of his Ryder Cup singles match in 1989. His unsuccessful attempts to move his ball from the front edge of a lake to the fairway would never have been made in stroke play. In his particular matchplay situation, he had little to lose. If he had taken his penalty stroke, he would still have lost the hole, and the match, to Jose-Maria Olazabal.

It is safest to make it your rule not to attempt to play a water shot unless at least half of your ball is exposed. But it also depends where your ball actually *is*.

The best advice is to pick and drop and forfeit one stroke. It could cost you more if you attempt these shots with a submerged ball.

The temptation may be to try and play this ball out but don't forget you got in the mess in the first place. So, realistically assess your chances of improving the situation from there.

You may have a playable lie from water but even the best players can make a hash of such shots.

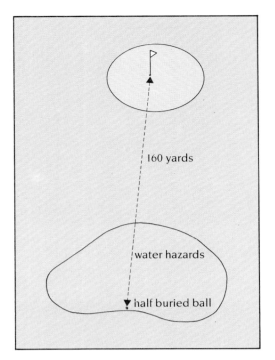

ABOVE: If you cannot reach the green it is sensible to drop out of the hazard for a 1 stroke penalty.

IN A STREAM

Here, you will usually be faced by a bank, so you need to get your ball up quickly. In this case, think along the same lines as you would if you were in a bunker. If you have strong doubts whether you can achieve enough height quickly enough to escape, don't try it. Accept your penalty stroke.

Your ball will usually be set upon a firm surface, sometimes small pebbles or gravel, and they could help, although they might chip your clubhead.

You'll be unfamiliar with playing from water, so it's essential to maintain confidence. Make up your mind how you're going to play your shot, and stick to your decision.

The club to use is often a sand iron, especially if you're actually swinging through water. It's the heaviest in your set, and has the most loft to help you get height quickly.

It's also worth weighing up the distance you are going to achieve. If you believe you can reach the green, for example, then go ahead. If, however, you are merely playing out, expecting to gain 20 yards or so, then there's little point in taking the risk. You'll be just as well off if you drop out under penalty, and hopefully, in a lie which will allow you to use a full 3-wood if you need maximum distance.

ABOVE AND RIGHT: The ball has to rise quickly.

Playing from a soft, wet lie –
but the ball isn't under water.

ABOVE: The ball is on a firm surface.

RIGHT: From a bad lie, could you be sure to clear this expanse of water? If not, take your penalty drop.

IN POND OR LAKE

In this situation, you may well be lying on soft mud, and in that case, you have to feel sure that you can get your clubhead under the ball. Hitting an inch or so behind the ball, as in a bunker shot, isn't likely to work, because your clubhead will simply bury itself in the ooze, and transfer little forward momentum to the ball.

From an expanse of water, you are unlikely to need a quickly rising shot – unless you have only just failed to carry the water and are on the far side. However, you will often find you need considerable length. If so, don't try it, because the chances of success are slight.

This ball is playable but, in view of the muddy conditions, make sure you have a towel handy ready to clean your face and clubs!

RULES AND CONDUCT WHEN IN WATER

The first thing to remember is that at no time must your club touch the water, at address or backswing. If it does, you lose one penalty stroke. The same applies anywhere in a water hazard, so be wary once you are inside the marked area, on a bank, for example.

You must also remember that a water hazard – lake, pond, stream, river or ditch – doesn't have to contain any water. The water hazard is the area marked as such. In theory, this could be any area; even a rough circle marked on a flat fairway could count as a water hazard.

Don't ground your club in a water hazard.

The red marker indicates this is a lateral water hazard and the rules governing it are different to those for a normal water hazard.

In real life, however, streams and the like can dry up in drought, just as lakes and ponds can, and the extent to which this happens often varies widely during a golfing year. Whatever the case, you are still in the water area if you are within the form of marking used – usually stakes.

But don't be too carelessly overjoyed if you find your ball in a water hazard but on dry land. Hazard rules still apply, and you will be penalised if you ground your club. If the ball is nestling in deep vegetation, you are not allowed to identify it, but as in sand, you are not penalised if you play the wrong ball, but immediately replay the shot.

The rules for natural loose impediments are just the same as those for sand. You may not move them. If, for example, a large branch prevents you playing your shot, you simply drop out of the hazard, under penalty.

A lateral water hazard doesn't only have to be in the form of a stream or river running alongside the fairway, it can be in the form of a pond.

A ditch, whether it contains water or not, is still defined as a water hazard.

ABOVE: Boarded banks define a water hazard clearly.

No water in sight, but this is still termed a water
hazard under the rules.

Casual water is any temporary accumulation on the course and is NOT a water hazard.

CASUAL WATER

Casual water is all water not normally a part of the course, and is usually the result of heavy rain, or even of an incursion by the sea. Being casual, it will not be marked as a hazard. You can lift and drop your ball without penalty from these unusual ground conditions.

You are also entitled to relief when you, rather than the ball, are in the water, when taking up your stance. The water doesn't have to be covering the surface. You can claim relief if water appears when your body weight causes it to rise and become visible around your shoes.

C H A P T E R   F O U R

OTHER HAZARDS

As the term suggests, bare lies occur when your ball is resting on the surface, without a covering of grass. It generally occurs on courses where there is more traffic than usual, or on small high spots where the grass dies off in dry weather.

Full shots ought to cause relatively little trouble, although of course, the ball is not 'sitting up' as so many golfers prefer for fairway wood shots. Many good players, however, prefer to use an iron from bare lies, or 'hard pan' as such lies are usually known in America and Australia. This is because there just isn't any grass between clubface and ball, making distance and the amount of backspin occurring, much more easy to predict.

For full shots with any club, from driver to sand iron, the best method is to make sure that you striking *down* on the ball. That's because there is less margin for error than if you attempt to sweep it away, as you might with a driver, for example. After all, the ball isn't sitting on a tee peg of grass.

To help you hit slightly downwards, move the ball back

in your stance, an inch or two further than you usually would for that particular club, and swing freely. Grip the club a little further down the shaft to help you achieve a more precise strike.

Shorter clubs are rather more difficult. When close to a green with an obstacle to clear – and even if there isn't one – most professionals reach for their sand iron, wanting maximum height and backspin. Unfortunately, you may find, when you address the ball, that the absence of that cushion of grass makes the trailing edge of the sand iron meet the ground before the leading edge does. At best, that means that it is difficult to get the leading edge under the ball. You may not think it, but however precise your stroke, you will meet the ball a little above the lowest point. The shot might just come off perfectly, but it isn't any too likely.

ABOVE: A sand iron is not appropriate on hard ground. The trailing edge of the iron would meet the ground first.

ABOVE: Strike down on the ball when it comes to rest on a bare lie, in this case re-seeded divots.

At worst, the trailing edge may meet the ground first, the club bounces, and the ball scuttles away on a low trajectory, right through the green.

However, there's an obvious answer to this problem. Set up for the shot with the ball further back in your stance, hands well ahead, until you find that the leading edge will meet the ground first.

Unfortunately, this delofts your sand iron. Unless you very much prefer using this club for this kind of shot, you may just as well modify your club selection and opt for a pitching wedge.

Whichever club you use, however, avoid a short backswing, which will almost certainly make you jab at the ball. The swing should be at least to shoulder height, and you should then gently accelerate the clubhead, making sure you don't slow down before impact.

Set your weight a little more on the front foot, and swing back steeply. Give yourself the feeling, as you come into the ball, that you are dropping the clubhead down to it.

A high spot.

TOP, ABOVE LEFT AND CENTRE: Chipping from a bare lie. The player was anxious and lifted his head too soon. The ball finished in the bunker to his right.

RIGHT: Here the shot is better and avoids the bunker.

BELOW: The ball is well back and the left wrist is still firm when the ball is well on its way.

DIVOT MARKS

On some holes, a high proportion of tee shots seem to come to rest in the same area – at the foot of a slope, or in a hollow, for example. The fairway will be heavily scarred by divots, in that area, and therefore, your chances of coming to rest in one are high.

One problem about this is that the head of your golf club may not fit into the divot mark, especially if you are thinking of playing a long iron. In that case, the rounded sole of a fairway wood might be a better option. If you don't need maximum distance, grip down the shaft and don't hit full out.

RIGHT: On extremely used patches of fairway, the ball is likely to come to rest in a divot.

LEFT: A long iron overlaps the divot mark.

You are likely to take some turf before you make contact, so play the ball back in your stance, with more weight on your front foot, than for a normal shot, and swing in steeply. Don't just punch your clubhead into the ground – keep it flowing through impact.

With the ball back in your stance, you can expect low flight, and consequently more run on the ball. This might not be a problem, unless you need to clear an obstacle such as a greenside bunker, and then want the ball to stop quickly.

If this is the case, you have a decision to make. If you are a good bunker player, you might even play for it, or accept the fact that your punch shot will finish far past the flag.

The alternative is to concentrate on exact striking, and play for a more normal shot, with the ball inside left heel, but play with a slightly open blade, break the wrists sharply on the backswing – creating a steep swing path – and swing back with a steeper path than usual.

Playing from a divot isn't usually particularly difficult, just so long as you take care. However, if the divot is deep, it may become impossible to achieve an ideal result. If so, accept it, and be content to do no more than play for a good position for your next shot.

ABOVE AND RIGHT: Playing out of a divot. Set the ball back in your stance and make sure you swing through. We have already told you how to avoid this shot but it is worth reiterating: replace all divots which you have made.

ABOVE AND RIGHT: Your ball may come to rest to the front or rear of a divot.

This is an unfortunate lie but you ought to get relief for unusual ground conditions. If not you could only hope to explode it out.

EXTREME STANCES

Having learned how to play all the shots with a normal stance on a flat lie, you rapidly discover that there are many occasions in a golfing year when you have to play from very uncomfortable positions. By 'uncomfortable' I don't mean stances which involve you in actual physical pain, such as having to back into a bush with cactus-like prickles, but those which arise when it's impossible to stand to the ball at all normally.

This normally involves standing with one foot on a vastly different level from the other.

There are various occasions when this might happen. Sometimes, an opponent, seeing the result of a less-than-perfect shot will comment how lucky you were not to have found sand – but this isn't always the case Often, being just not quite in the sand will put you in a more difficult situation that actually finding yourself in it. Playing with one foot in a bunker and the other out, is never easy, and the deeper the bunker, the more difficult it is.

Much the same situation arises when you aren't quite in a water hazard. With luck, you won't have to get your feet wet, because you can find a foot placement on the bank, but you still have that very uneven stance.

Balls that miss greens leaving you short, or to either side, often finish on banks, most times leaving you with an uphill shot. Those that run through the putting surface may well find a bank at the back, presenting you with a downhill shot.

Although these situations *seem* very different, in the end, they give rise to the same range of extreme stances. The ball can be either well above or well below your feet, or your two feet can be at very different levels.

ABOVE: Both feet in a bunker isn't an easy situation. Grip right down the shaft.

RIGHT AND OPPOSITE: You must limit your ambition playing with feet at different levels.

UP A STEEP BANK

Here, it won't often be very difficult to balance, and the fact that the back of the ball will usually be exposed is also helpful: you might even be able to see the very bottom of it. As steep banks usually occur near greens, it's unlikely that you will have to use much power. But there are occasions which disprove this rule. You might, for example, hit a wild tee shot and finish up among dunes on a link course, or some artful architect may even have contrived some humps for you.

Because of the slope, most of your weight will be thrown on the back foot. You can live with that, providing you only need a fairly gentle swing. Set up with the ball towards your front foot, and don't forget that you'll need to judge the loft of the club needed. Anything at all straight faced is likely to knock your ball straight into the turf, because of the severe slope in front of the ball. Keep your body out of the shot, and visualise yourself playing almost entirely with a hands-and-arms action. Rehearse the shot to see how to maintain balance.

ABOVE: Not too difficult to maintain balance even on this steep slope – as long as you don't need a full swing.

Often, the sand iron will be the club to use because you will get quick height from it, and that steep slope behind the ball means that there is no danger of the sole flange catching the ball and bouncing.

When attempting longer shots, however, you won't want to use the sand iron, because you'll get so little length from it. How far you can move the ball depends on your ability to maintain your balance as you increase swing speed.

A practice swing or two will tell you how far you can go – and if you fall over, then you'd better decrease both your swing speed and your ambitions.

These ought to be fairly limited, anyway, and on very severe slopes, you can't expect to wind up your body and still retain balance. Stick to hands-and-arms action, with not too much shoulder and hip turn. Also remember to allow for the fact that you'll get more height than usual with the club you select.

ABOVE: Dunes on a links course.

DOWN A STEEP BANK

This is a far more difficult proposition. Take the tricky matter of balance.

Any reasonably vigorous shot will force you to transfer your weight wholly to the front foot, which may already be finding it difficult to find a firm foothold on that steep slope. You are certain to topple forwards – not that that's any real problem, just so long as you've got the ball away first.

Getting at the back of the ball on a steep downslope can be a very severe problem. The situation is exactly the converse to the one faced on upslopes, because the geometry is against you. That downslope actually shields the back of the ball.

First, set up the ball well back in your stance. Depending on the severity of the slope, this can be very far back indeed – even behind your right foot. This helps you come down sharply on the ball, and to get into the back of it. You will also need to pick the club up sharply on the backswing, and chop steeply down on the ball.

Because you have the ball so far back in your stance, you are, in effect, delofting the club you use by many degrees. But don't be tempted to use the sand iron, because of the very great danger of bouncing the sole off the turf before meeting the ball. Do remember that, whichever club you choose, you will get a much lower flight trajectory, and so you can only use the lofted irons. Don't even think about using anything less than your 8-iron. If you do, you'll probably achieve no more than scuttling your ball along the ground.

When the ball is well below your feet, you must overcome a strong tendency to slice.

BALL BELOW THE FEET

Here, the ball is also a good deal further away from you than normal. To get yourself nearer, you have to 'sit down to it' and also grip the club right at the end. As with all shots from severe slopes, you won't be able to make any real body turn, and particularly in this stance, that means a very strong tendency to slice. You can, however, aim off to allow for this left-to-right movement.

Your tendency to topple towards the ball must be resisted, but even an increased lean towards the ball increases the danger of shanking. Think, while you swing, that you mustn't bring this part of the club into the ball. Concentrate on bringing the centre of the club face into it.

BALL ABOVE THE FEET

Here we have the reverse situation, but most players find it's an easier one to play, perhaps because the player is nearer to the ball. Anything which reduces the hand and eye co-ordination in a golf shot ought to make it easier.

This time, grip the club lower; when the ball is very much above your feet, you may even have to have the right hand off the grip and on the shaft. When you have to go this far, the question arises about what to do with the handle of the club.

There is a tendency for it to want to disappear into your stomach. The answer is to place your ball well forward in your stance, so that the handle now avoids your stomach, and projects beyond your left hip. It will still be in the way, but this is an awkward shot and you have to make the most of your possibilities to make a moderate – not a great – shot.

The tendency is to hook, although playing with the ball so far forward does reduce this danger. Again, allow for right-to-left movement of the ball by aiming off. You should get a low flight, and consequently, more run on dry ground.

In all these slope situations, we have been considering severe problems. Don't be over-ambitious: aim for a result that gets you into a more favourable position.

Grip the club lower when the ball is above your feet. Most players find this an easier shot to play than the opposite situation because they are nearer the ball.

RESTRICTED BACKSWINGS

Wayward shots will often get you into situations where you can't swing back freely. If you're among trees, for example, a branch may impede the top of your swing. If you are really close up to a tree, you may have no room to swing at all.

Consider the alternatives. One option is to take a penalty drop. Another, is to play away from your target, aiming to get into a position where you have an open shot to the flag. You can also consider playing the shot left-handed, toe down. Yet another method is to play one-handed: this means turning your back on the target, and striking with the full face of the club.

Of these, only playing away from the target offers an easy shot. Most golfers don't practise them, but it's always possible to compensate for inexperience, to some extent, by rehearsing the shot a few times. You then carry out the shot you've rehearsed, and try to maintain your confidence. Above all do not change your shot in mid-swing, perhaps in an effort to force another 20 yards. The result is more likely to be stubbing the club into the ground, or even an air shot. You would have been far better off taking your medicine in the form of a penalty shot.

If you aren't playing through rough, don't forget your putter. It's the easiest club in the bag to use, especially one-handed, or with an unaccustomed grip.

So far, the discussion has been about extremely restricted backswings, or perhaps no space at all. It's far more usual, however, to get into situations where you have only to deal with limited restriction, as when your club would be impeded by a bush, or the lower branches of a tree.

Test out how severe the impediment is. Remember, you are not allowed to improve your position by repeatedly swinging into the obstruction, so you can't break twigs until the problem is eliminated. That costs penalty strokes.

You are, however, allowed to rehearse your stroke, just so long as you do not cause breakages. Quite frequently, you will be able to play a full stroke, when you find that there isn't anything of real substance in the way. Even so, it's all too easy to lose confidence at the last moment and make a badly timed shot.

On balance, it's better to take no chances. If you feel that your confidence isn't high enough, shorten the backswing so that you don't reach the obstruction, and rehearse your swing once again. Once more, do play the shot you've rehearsed. Don't be tempted, in an effort to gain just a few yards more, force your clubhead at the ball with a thrust of the hands. This will ruin the timing of the shot, and as likely as not, produce a total mis-hit.

The branches will restrict your backswing so rehearse your swing.

OPPOSITE TOP LEFT: Only a little jab is possible in this situation.

OPPOSITE TOP RIGHT: If the backswing is totally restricted you can only drop the ball under penalty. In the bottom picture, local rules may permit the drop without penalty.

ABOVE AND OPPOSITE: When playing awkward shots with obstructions in the way, practice the shot a couple of times first to find out how restricted you are in your swing and follow through. When you feel ready and have a mental picture of the shot in your mind, then play it.

UNUSUAL SURFACES

On a golf course, you expect to be playing from grass. You won't often be disappointed, but there are exceptions. Let's think of an area of the Old Course at St Andrews, where there are two famous 'hazards' in the shape of roads.

One is called 'Grannie Clark's Wynd', a right of way, dating from time immemorial, crossing the first and last fairways, running from the town to the sea. A good shot from the tee at the par 4 1st hole will land well beyond it, but this isn't the case at the 18th. The other is the famous metalled track which gave the 17th its world-renowned name of 'The Road Hole'. It runs along the right of the fairway, and, then tight along the right-hand edge of the green.

If a good player's ball comes to rest on Grannie Clark's Wynd, he won't be much disturbed. He'll simply select his wedge or a 9-iron and pitch to the hole. The other road doesn't create much of a problem either. He can play off the road towards the flag, but may have great difficulty stopping his ball in time, if he tries to lob to the green. He can also roll the ball up the grassy slope between road and green, but will find it hard to get the right distance.

At club level, however, most golfers are quite bothered enough just at the thought of playing off a road surface, never mind finishing close to the flag.

BELOW AND OPPOSITE: The danger when playing off a road or gravel path is the possible damage to your club. However, shortening your hold should reduce the possibility of club damage.

So what should you do in this situation? First of all, study the local rules. You may find that you are allowed to drop off without penalty, and would choose to do so. You can also decide that a ball is unplayable, wherever you like, and drop off under penalty – that's if the local rules tell you that the road in question is part of the golf course.

Really though – this is just a little cowardly. As I've said, professionals facing this situation will play the ball as it lies with scarcely a pause for thought: the shot isn't really very difficult, though it does need precise striking.

Choose a club which will give you the right distance without forcing the shot, and grip it a little shorter. Swing smoothly, and you should get a good result. This is also important because of the very real danger of club damage. Swinging a club violently into contact with such an unforgiving surface could well mean a chip out of the leading edge of your iron, or the shaft may break off at the hosel. You can reduce your chances of this damage by not swinging full out – If your iron shots usually take a large divot after the ball, you will need a change of approach to avoid almost certain mayhem, and also prevent jarring of hands and wrists. The pro will try to nip the ball off the surface cleanly, knowing that he can rely on the loft of his club to give him backspin. You should do likewise, aiming to get the bottom of the blade under the ball, and then travelling along a line parallel with the hard surface, not into it. This way, you should clip the ground, not crack into it.

Before you play the shot off a difficult surface check the local rules, you may be entitled to a drop without penalty.

INDEX

Italic page numbers refer to illustrations.

A

Animals
scrapes and holes made by 39
Augusta National 32

B

Backspin
bunker shots 20, 22
flyers 49, *49*
Backswing
restricted 88, *88, 89*
Ball
above the feet 87, *87*
below the feet 86, *86*
moving 58, *58*
playing wrong 39
searching for, bunker shots 39
unplayable 43, *59*
Ballesteros, Severiano 32, 49
Banks
playing down 85
playing up 84–5
Bare lie 74–6
bunkers 30, *31*
chipping from *77*
sand iron 75, *75, 76*
The Belfry 63
Bunkers 8–39, *83*
animals, scrapes and holes made by 39
backspin 20, 22
bare lies 30, *31*, 38
buried lies 22–3

catching the sand behind the ball 35
chip shots 14–15
club arc 16
clubhead speed *23*
depth 34
downhill lie 26, *26*
face 35
failure to escape from 14
fairway bunkers 32, *32, 33*, 34, *34*
firm sand 14–15
5-irons 35
free drop 39
grass banks 38
grass islands *36*, 39
greenside 12, *12*, 14–15, 32
grounding clubs *36*, 38–39
"GUR" 39
height of shot *16, 17, 18, 25, 29*
identifying balls 39
long shots from 18, *18, 19*
low flight shots 23
man-made objects in *38*
9-iron used in 20, *20*
overhanging lip of turf 29, *29, 35, 35*
pot bunkers 32, *33*
practice *37*
raking the sand *36*, 38
recovery shots 35, *35*
rehearsing shots 28
repairs to 39
rules and behaviour in 36, 38–9
sand irons 8–10, *9*

searching for balls 39
7-iron 32
short shots from 18
splash shot *11*, 14, *15*
stance 16, *21, 23*, 28, *28*, 35
steep face 23, *23*
stones, removal of *38*, 39
thinning the shot 35
3-wood 35, *35*
timber shoring 39
uneven sand 30, *31*
uphill lie 27, *27*
wedge used in 20
wet sand 14–15, 20
wrong ball, playing 39
Buried lies
bunker shots 22–3
rough 43, *43*

C

Calcavecchia, Mark 32
Casper, Billy 42
Casual water 73, *73*
Chipping
bare lies *77*
from bunkers 14–15
loose material, removal of 55
Clubs
choosing 8
cleaning 49, *49*
deep rough 41–2, *41*
driver 44
8-iron 85
5-iron 35, 46
irons 46, *46, 47*, 79
lofted *44*
9-iron 20, *20, 43*
putter 8

sand iron 8–10, *9*, 41–2, *41, 44*, 64, *75, 75*, 76
7-iron 32, *45*, 46
6-iron 46
3-wood 35, *35*, 64
wedge 20, *43*, 44
woods 44, *45*, 46, *46*, 79

D

Deep rough 41–2, *41, 42*
Ditches 69, *71*
Divots
divot marks 79–80, *79, 80, 81*
re-seeded *75*
replacing *55*
Driver 44
Dual purpose sand iron 10
Dunes *85*

E

8-iron *85*

F

Fairway bunkers
deep 34
pot bunkers 32, *33*
5-iron
playing from bunkers 35
playing from the rough 46
Fleck, Jack 43
Flyers 49
Free drop
bunker shots 39

G

Greenside